JAGUAR

JAGUAR
THE KING OF THE CATS

by
LINDA CRAVEN
and
JERRY CRAVEN

THE ROURKE CORPORATION, INC.
Vero Beach, FL 32964

Cover photograph: the Jaguar XK140 classic roadster.

ACKNOWLEDGMENTS

We are grateful to Jaguar, Ltd. for supplying the photographs for this book. We are especially grateful to Mr. Arnold Bolton for his assistance and advice about Jaguar.

© 1991 The Rourke Corporation, Inc.

Library of Congress Cataloging-in-Publication Data

Craven, Linda.
    Jaguar: the king of the cats / by Linda Craven and Jerry Craven.
       p. cm. – (Car classics)
    Includes index.
    Summary: Gives a brief history of Jaguar cars and describes some classic models.
    ISBN 0-86593-144-5
    1. Jaguar automobile – Juvenile literature. [1. Jaguar automobile.] I. Craven, Jerry. II. Title. III. Series.
TL215.J3C73 1991

                                      91-7645
                                        CIP
                                         AC

JAGUAR

CONTENTS

CHAPTER 1

THE FAST CATS: RACING AT LE MANS

This Silk Cut racer won the 1988 24-hour race at Le Mans.

The Le Mans track in France consists of just over eight miles of sharply curved road. Here the world's best racers go up against one another in a grueling 24-hour race. The cars stop only for fuel, for quick repairs, and to change drivers. The race tests both speed and endurance.

In 1951, a Jaguar XK120 placed first at Le Mans. By 1953, Jaguar C-type roadsters dominated the Le Mans race. C-type Jaguars took first, second, and fourth places. The first-place car averaged over 100 miles per hour.

JAGUAR

Jaguar's next roadster, the D-type, had a more powerful engine than the C-type and a body design that cut wind resistance better. The D-type won the Le Mans in 1955, 1956, and 1957.

Jaguar's early victories at Le Mans surprised the world because the winning C-types and D-types were all regular production cars, not cars built just for racing. These were sports cars right off the assembly line. Any ordinary driver could buy and use them because they had no special modifications that would make them unsuitable for driving in traffic.

Years after the early victories, Jaguar re-entered serious racing at Le Mans with the Silk Cut. Unlike the C-type and D-type winners, the Silk Cut was not a roadster but a car designed only for speed and endurance. The Silk Cut won at Le Mans in 1988 and 1990.

Jaguar built the D-type for both street and race track.

CHAPTER 2

THE EARLY FAST CATS

Jaguar has been building some of the fastest cars in the world since before World War II. Way back in 1935, the Jaguar SS90 could go 90 miles per hour, and the 1938 model SS100 went even faster.

Jaguar's fast cats have always been a combination of current technology and traditional building materials. For example, Jaguar engineers built their early roadster, the XK120, on a wooden frame. Most early car builders got their start as makers of horse-drawn wooden coaches, so manufacturers kept the tradition of using hardwood frames well into the twentieth century. Although Jaguar stopped using wooden frames, it still decorates the interior of its cars with wood.

Early models of the XK120 were built on a wooden frame.

The Jaguar C-type won the 1951 Le Mans endurance race.

Jaguar made its first XK120 roadsters with aluminum bodies to avoid having to invest in steel presses. When the XK120 became popular enough to be mass-produced, Jaguar turned it into an all-steel car, frame and body. The XK120 was named for its speed: it could go just over 120 miles per hour.

The XK120 made an impressive showing in the 1950 Le Mans. William Lyons, the chief executive officer of Jaguar, helped redesign the XK120 into the C-type Jaguar, winner of the 1951 Le Mans. The C-type was the first great Jaguar racer that could also be driven by the ordinary person in normal traffic.

CHAPTER 3

FROM SIDECAR TO MOTORCAR: FROM BIRD TO CAT

It all began in an old shed in England. William Walmsley had a motorcycle. He wanted to be able to take passengers, so he built a sidecar and attached it to his motorcycle. Later, a twenty-year-old neighbor suggested that the two go into business making sidecars.

The neighbor, William Lyons, became the head of the company, which grew into the maker of the fastest and most famous cars in the world. Jaguar builds its cars in Coventry, England (see map on facing page).

The company that became Jaguar started out building motorcycle sidecars, like the one shown here. These were called Swallows.

The early cars made by Jaguar were called Swallows. This is a 1931 SS1 Swallow roadster.

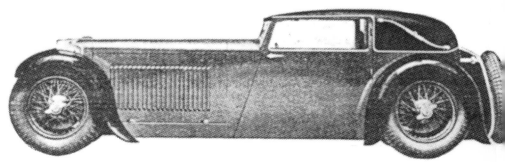

JAGUAR

Drivers praised the early SS1 Swallow sedan for its sleek design.

Jaguars are assembled in a factory located in Coventry, in the heart of England.

The motorcycle sidecar looked like a rocket. Its design cut down wind resistance and allowed the motorcycle to move faster. Lyons named it the Swallow after a sleek, fast bird.

Before long, the Swallow Sidecar Company began making car bodies, as did several other companies in England in the 1920s. Coach builders, as these companies were called, made car bodies to fit on the frame, or chassis, of cars manufactured by other companies. The Swallow coach, or car body, fit on an Austin, and the car was sold as an Austin Swallow. Swallow also made some bodies for Fiat.

In 1931, Swallow came out with its own car, the SS1. By 1934, the SS cars were so popular that the company had stopped building coaches for other cars, and Swallow changed its name to Jaguar to associate the car with a sleek, powerful cat.

From the first, Jaguar made both sports cars and larger four-door sedans. The English call sports cars roadsters, and they call sedans saloons.

9

CHAPTER 4

WHAT POWERS A CAT?

*The Jaguar
2900 cc engine.*

During the last part of World War II, while the Jaguar employees spent more time putting out fires from Nazi bombing raids than making war material, William Lyons and his chief engineers began designing a new engine to make Jaguars run faster and smoother than ever. The design was good enough to be used in Jaguars for the next 38 years.

American-made cars measure engine size in cubic inches. The English use the metric system and measure engine size in cubic centimeters (cc). Engine size refers to the total space inside the cylinders when the pistons are pressed down. The larger the total space, the more powerful the engine.

The big V-12 engine in many Jaguars today was first used in the Jaguar XJ13 in 1966.

*The powerful Jaguar
V-12 engine.*

The experimental XJ13 was a refinement of the D-type.

The XJ13 was an experimental car, and only one of its type was ever built. Its revolutionary V-12 engine had a 4994 cc capacity in two banks of cylinders. The body design of the XJ13 was a refinement of the D-type.

Jaguar never entered the XJ13 in competitive racing. It is on display today in a Jaguar showroom along with an original Swallow Sidecar and other company classics.

CHAPTER 5

THE FACTORY: BUILDING A CAT

Dropping the car body into place.

Jaguar has three factories in England. The factory in Birmingham builds the car bodies. The Rockford plant in Coventry builds the engines, suspensions and axles. The third plant, also in Coventry, hand crafts the upholstery and the wood pieces, and assembles the cars. Designers at the Whitely Center in Coventry plan Jaguars of the future.

In 1990, Jaguar produced about 50,000 cats. About three-fourths of all Jaguars made are exported from England to other countries. The majority, about 40 percent, go to buyers in the United States.

Every Jaguar is made to order according to the customer's preferences. Each has a "birth certificate." As the car is assembled, careful records are kept to show which craftsmen cut, shaped, fitted, and assembled each part.

If you ordered a Jaguar today, you could choose the color of the leather, the color and type of wood, the color of the body paint, carpet, and other special features. And since each car is made to order, it would be about three months before your new car would be completed and delivered.

Installing the XJ5 engine.

Assembling the Jaguar XJS according to customer order.

CHAPTER 6

CAT CRAFTSMANSHIP

Kings, sultans, and presidents choose Jaguar for its quality craftsmanship.

The workers in the Jaguar plant are among the most skillful in the world. They take care to make sure each car runs well, functions properly, and is as beautiful as the sleek cat for which the car is named.

Craftsmen take great pride in producing an automobile purchased by presidents, kings and queens, business executives, sultans, and collectors world over.

Master craftsmen work their way up at Jaguar. At the leather cutting tables, where 117 pieces must be cut for each car, craftsmen have worked for Jaguar an average of 22 years.

Leather workers use only the finest cowhides.

While most car makers use vinyl or other man-made fabrics for seats, doors and headliners, Jaguar uses only cowhide leather. Each hide is selected carefully. Three hides are required for one Jaguar, and all three must match in color, texture, and thickness.

The woodworkers select only the most beautiful wood grains for the dash, console, and door panels. The wood, usually burr walnut from California or Europe, is cut precisely so that the wood grain on one side of the car is a mirror image of that on the other.

Wood workers match grain to form a mirror image.

CHAPTER 7

DESIGNING A CAT

Today, car designers make use of computer-assisted graphics, but it was not always so.

In the early years of Jaguar, William Lyons described to workers what he thought the car should look like. They built models from wood, metal, and clay. Then Lyons pointed to places he wanted changed, and the workers revised the models. When it looked the way Lyons wanted it, the car design was complete.

Computer-assisted graphics allow today's designers to place drawings on the computer screen and then view them from any angle. They make changes on the screen until a desired design is complete.

Jaguar artists develop many major body designs, but only three become clay models. The best two are then built in fiberglass. Only one design becomes a functioning prototype. Jaguar tested almost 100 prototypes of the XJ40 for five million miles in different road conditions. The test sites included:

❏ Northern Ontario in winter, where the cars were outfitted with special front and rear panels to disguise their Jaguar identity. Two prototype XJ cars ran around-the-clock during the winter of 1983.

❏ Phoenix, Arizona, where air temperature reached 122 degrees Fahrenheit.

❏ The rough roads of the Australian outback.

Given all the steps in design and testing, it's no wonder it takes years for Jaguar to produce a new model.

Today, Jaguar designers make use of computers.

Designers made the XJS look like a car of the future.

CHAPTER 8

TESTS FOR THE BEST

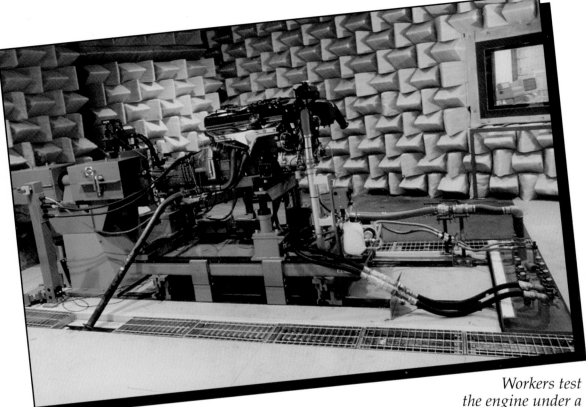

*Workers test
the engine under a
variety of conditions.*

Jaguar engineers want to be sure every car put on the road is the best car it can be. They have developed an elaborate system of inspection, testing, and quality assurance.

Every piece and part that goes into a Jaguar is examined by an experienced inspector. The engine and many other working parts are also tested by computer. A water test checks for water seepage in the trunk (called the boot, in England) and into the hood (called the bonnet). A computerized rolling road test is performed in the factory. Finally, during an open road test of each car, technicians check for wind and road noise and other possible problems.

Jaguar makers do not stop with factory tests. They want to be sure their cars continue to perform perfectly for their new car owners. Jaguar has designed a computer diagnostic test system for use by service representatives all over the world. The computerized system makes maintenance and repairs more scientific. A skilled mechanic can use it to diagnose and pinpoint any problems that develop. The computer system is available in several languages, including Dutch, French, German, Italian, Spanish, and, of course, English.

Safety testing is an important part of assembling the cars.

CHAPTER 9

HOW FAST IS A CAT?

The XK150 on a British street in 1957.

DISTANCE COVERED PER CAR
24 Consecutive Hours of Racing
in the 1953 Le Mans
One Lap = 8.38 miles

PLACE	DRIVERS	MILES
1. Jaguar XK120	Rolt and Hamilton	2,540.3
2. Jaguar XK120	Moss and Walker	2,511.2
3. Cunningham	Walters and Fitch	2,498.2
4. Jaguar XK120	Whitehead and Stewart	2,486.1
5. Ferrari	Marzotto and Marzotto	2,458.6

The 1990 Jaguar Silk Cut raced to victory at Le Mans.

Jaguar has always been famous for both its speed and its body styling. Some notable achievements in moving fast:

1949   A Jaguar XK120 was clocked in Belgium at 132.6 miles per hour (mph). *Autocar* magazine observed at the time that such speeds were impossible in England because there were no roads capable of handling cars traveling at that speed.

1950   A Jaguar XK120 set a world record by averaging 107.46 mph for 24 hours of driving.

1952   An XK120 produced on the assembly line with no special changes was clocked at a Belgium race track at an average speed of 172.412 mph.

1957   An XK150 roadster went from 0 to 100 mph in 14 seconds.

1986   The new Jaguar XJ40 sedan (not a sports car) went from 0 to 60 mph in 7.4 seconds.

1988   The Jaguar Silk Cut racer won at Le Mans with an average speed of 137.65 mph.

1990   The Jaguar Silk Cut racer again won at Le Mans.

CHAPTER 10

CLASSIC CATS

MARK VII

Beauty, grace, and speed all reached their peak in the classic Jaguar Mark VII. This car was introduced at motor shows in London and New York in 1950 and immediately became popular.

The largest and heaviest of the sedans (3,808 pounds), the Mark VII was 10 feet in length, about the same as many American luxury cars of the time. But at 6 feet 1 inch, it was wider. It also had less overhanging weight, so it handled better. It had a maximum speed of 103 mph and a 0 – 60 mph acceleration time of 13.4 seconds.

The Mark VII proved itself at the Monte Carlo races in a series of wins in the 1950s. The Mark VII's torque (rotary force in the engine) was so good that it could plough through the deep snow drifts of the rally. The Mark VII also won the Silverstone Production Car Race in 1953.

The classic Jaguar Mark VII offered both comfort and speed.

THE FABULOUS E-TYPE

Because a group of Jaguar engineers didn't want to waste the company's large surplus of D-type parts, they pieced together a new roadster out of spare parts.

The result was the E-type, the fastest and perhaps most famous sports car in the world. It could accelerate from 0 to 60 miles per hour in 6.8 seconds and could reach a speed of 150 mph. It averaged 17 miles per gallon of gas, an amazing feat in the early 1960s.

The original E-type had a 6-cylinder engine. Later models had the V-12. The last E-type was made in 1974.

The E-type was the fastest sports car of the 1960s.

CHAPTER 11

BIG CAT LUXURY: CONTEMPORARY SEDANS

THE XJ6

The luxurious XJ6 is outfitted with state of the art technological wizardry. It's available with the 2.9 liter engine or the more powerful 4.0 liter unit. Outfitted with a manual gearbox, it can accelerate from 0 to 60 mph in 7.1 seconds. It can go 140 mph.

It also has power-assisted rack and pinion steering (the steering column is adjustable), anti-lock disc brakes, and a computerized instrument panel. You know you're in an XJ6 when you relax with a built-in driver's footrest, turn on your remote control outside mirror heaters, and use your heated windshield washers.

The 1990 Jaguar XJ6 has many luxuries, including heated door mirrors.

*Called a Daimler
in England, the
Vanden Plas is the
top-of-the-line Jaguar.*

THE VANDEN PLAS

In England, the top-of-the line Jaguar sedan is called the Daimler. In the United States, it's sold as the Vanden Plas.

You could say the Vanden Plas is loaded. It has a 6-cylinder 4.0 liter engine and an automatic transmission. You'd never be cold starting up this beauty – the front seats are electrically heated for cold winter days.

The back seat passengers can use their separate reading lamps and pull down the picnic tables in front of them. And all riders enjoy the six-speaker audio system.

The double-six saloon (sedan) has a 5.3 liter V-12 engine. Even at speeds of nearly 140 mph, this cat purrs almost silently.

CHAPTER 12

COLLECTORS' CATS

THE XKSS

The flashy XKSS was a street-wise version of the D-type racer. It was equipped with tiny slim-line bumpers, a full-width windshield, silencers, and lighting suitable for road use. Only a few of these beauties were built. They're now collectors' items with a high price tag.

Jaguar built only a few of the classy XKSS models. Now they are collectors' items.

THE MARK II

The greatest of all the sedans that were raced was the Mark II. Wire wheels were used when racing to help cool the hard-pressed brakes. If you were the owner of this big cat, you could expect it to accelerate from 0 – 60 mph in 8.5 seconds and run flat out at 125 mph.

Wire wheels helped cool the brakes on the Mark II.

THE MARK IX

The Mark IX was the last Jaguar sedan built on a separate chassis. It was one of the first with power steering, making a large, heavy car easier to handle. The Mark IX carried its great weight with dignity at 114 mph.

Many consider the Mark IX to be in a class by itself for beauty of design.

THE XJS

Convertibles are popular in every age. Sports car fans especially loved the convertible XJS Jaguar for its design and its powerful V-12 engine that could move the car fast enough to leave other motorists in the dust.

Mark II, 3.8 liter (1962)

Engine

Type	In-line, water-cooled
No. of cylinders	6
Bore/stroke mm	87 x 106
Displacement cc	3781
Valve operation	Twin overhead camshafts
Sparkplugs per cyl.	1
Compression ratio	9:1
Carburetion	2 SU 1.75 in. carburetors

Drive Train

Clutch	Single dry plate
Transmission	Four-speed and reverse (automatic optional)

The XJS is a small car with a big V-12 engine.

CHAPTER 13

FUTURE CATS

A new era of Jaguar began in early 1990. Impressed with its long record of excellence, Ford of Britain purchased controlling interest. Ford now owns Jaguar.

Jaguar still remains separate from the parent company and retains its traditional standards of excellence in craftsmanship. The money from the Ford purchase has made possible the use of new technologies to improve the design, engineering, and production at Jaguar.

Two new models will probably be added in the near future – a smaller sports car and a smaller sedan. The company also plans to increase production to between 150,000 and 200,000 Jaguars per year by the year 2000.

The Jaguar XJS convertible is a result of years of development and design.

*Many regard
the XJ220
as a prototype
for the future.*

The futuristic XJ220 may prove to be a prototype of sports cars for the twenty-first century. The XJ220 is, according to the company, "the fastest road-going Jaguar to date." The 3.5 liter, twin turbo, V-6 engine accelerates to 100 miles per hour in just eight seconds. Its maximum speed is over 200 miles per hour.

Jaguar has made its place in the world. And, like the big cat that it is, it promises to leap forward into the future, sleek, powerful, and full of grace.

*Fine wood and leather
interiors have remained
popular among Jaguar
owners from the beginning
to the present day.*

CHAPTER 14

JAGUAR: IMPORTANT DATES

1920 William Walmsley begins making sidecars in his shed.

1922 Walmsley and neighbor, William Lyons, start the Swallow Sidecar Company in Blackpool, England.

1926 Lyons expands to coach building and moves to a larger building.

1927 The Austin Swallow two-seater is announced in *Autocar* magazine.

1928 The factory moves to Coventry and again expands.

1931 The SS range of models is introduced.

1934 The name Jaguar is added to Swallow.

1941-1945 Car production stops during the war; the company makes war material.

1945 Jaguar engineers develop the XK engine, used in Jaguars for the next 38 years; car manufacturing resumes.

1949 XK120 cars finish first and second in the race at Silverstone.

1950 The XK120 wins the Alpine Trial and Ulster TT race. The Mark VII is a hit at the London Car Show.

1951 The XK 120C (C-type) wins at Le Mans.

1952 An XK 120 coupe averages over 100 mph for a week, breaking world speed records.

1953 C-type Jaguars are victorious at Le Mans.

1955 D-types win at Le Mans.

1956 William Lyons is knighted by the Queen and is now known as "Sir William Lyons." The Mark VII wins at Monte Carlo.

1957 A D-type gives Jaguar its fifth win at Le Mans.

1959 The Mark II is introduced with a choice of 2.4, 3.4 or 3.8 liter engine.

1961 The sensational E-type roadster and the big Mark X are introduced.

1966 The experimental XJ13 introduces a Jaguar V-12 engine.

1968 The XJ6 wins high praises in the auto world.

1975 The last E-type deliveries are made.

1986 The XJ40 is announced and wins the "Top Car" Award from the Guild of Motoring Writers.

1988 The Jaguar Silk Cut wins at Le Mans.

1990 The Silk Cut again wins at Le Mans.

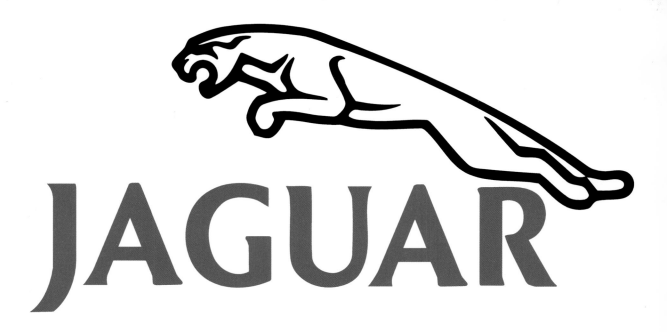

The Jaguar logo suggests both power and grace.

GLOSSARY

axle – The shaft or crossbar on which the wheels are mounted and on which they turn.

computer-assisted graphics – Using a computer for drawing or designing objects.

coupe (koop) – A two-door automobile.

cylinder – The part of an engine in which a piston moves up and down to create power.

mph – Miles per hour. The speed of a car in miles per hour.

prototype – A first or original model.

quality assurance – A system of maintaining high grade work.

roadster – A sports car made for normal driving use but capable of high speeds.

sedan (suh-DAN) – A four-door car, called saloon in England.

suspension – The springs and other flexible parts of the car used to absorb shocks and make the car ride more smoothly.

INDEX